Co-published by agreement between Shi Tu Hui and World Book, Inc.

Shi Tu Hui
Room 1807, Block 1,
#3 West Dawang Road
Chaoyang District, Beijing 100025
P.R. China

World Book, Inc.
180 North LaSalle Street
Suite 900
Chicago, Illinois 60601
USA

Library of Congress Cataloging-in-Publication Data for this volume has been applied for.

True or False? (set #4)
ISBN: 978-0-7166-5417-9 (set, hc.)

Volcanoes
ISBN: 978-0-7166-5427-8 (hc.)

Also available as:
ISBN: 978-0-7166-5437-7 (e-book)
ISBN: 978-0-7166-5447-6 (soft cover)

Staff

Executive Committee

President
Geoff Broderick

Vice President, Editorial
Tom Evans

Vice President, Finance
Molly Stedron

Vice President, International and Marketing
Eddy Kisman

Vice President, Technology and Operations
Jason Dole

Director, Human Resources
Bev Ecker

Editorial

Writer
William D. Adams

Manager, New Content
Jeff De La Rosa

Associate Manager, New Content
William D. Adams

Curriculum Designer
Caroline Davidson

Proofreader
Nathalie Strassheim

Graphics and Design

Coordinator, Design Development & Production:
Brenda Tropinski

Senior Visual Communications Designer
Melanie Bender

Senior Media Editor
Rosalia Bledsoe

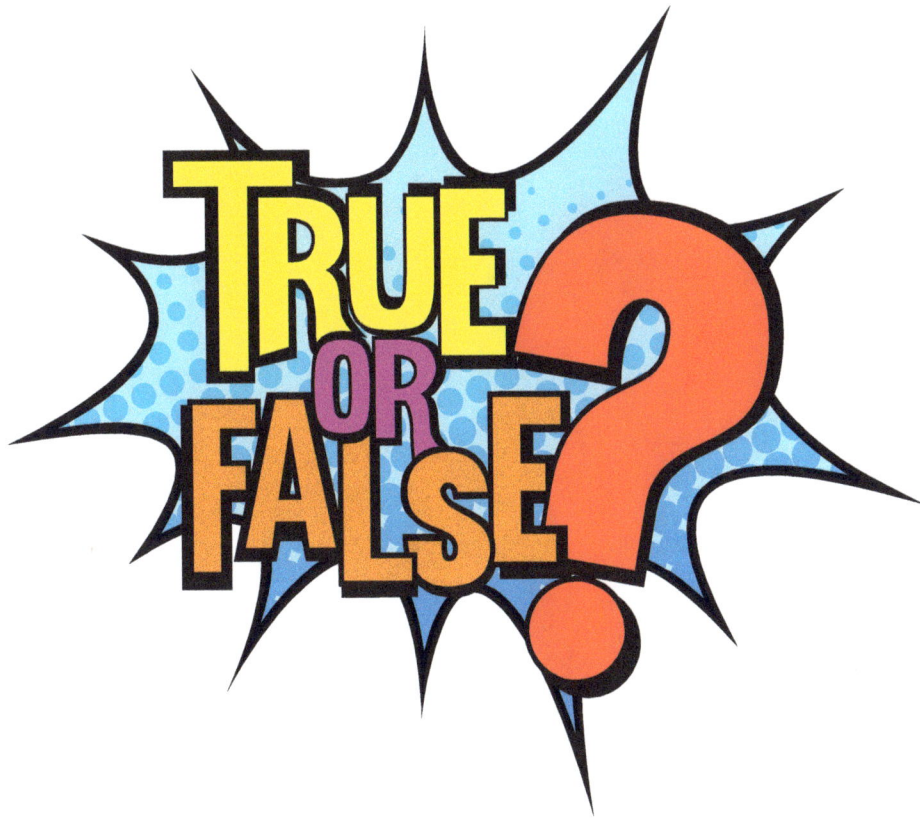

TRUE OR FALSE?

VOLCANOES

WORLD BOOK

www.worldbook.com

TRUE OR FALSE?

All volcanoes are cone-shaped mountains of rock that erupt lava.

5

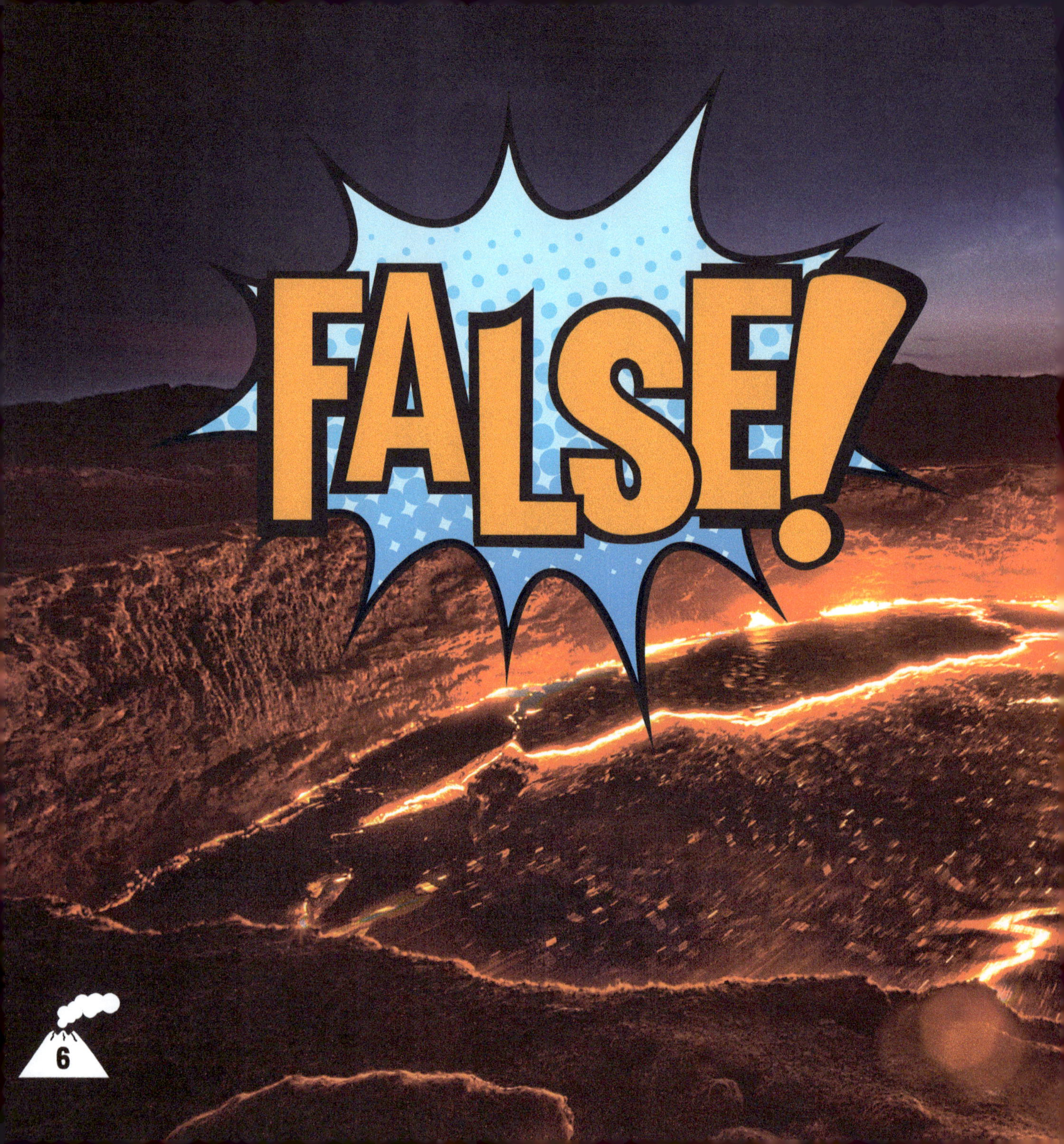
FALSE!

A volcano is any place where *magma* (molten rock from deep underground) erupts onto the surface. Volcanoes can take the form of mountainlike *stratovolcanoes*, gently sloped *shield volcanoes*, and many other shapes. Some volcanoes erupt large amounts of lava, but others erupt mostly ash and gases.

TRUE OR FALSE?

Volcanoes are named after the Roman god of fire.

9

10

TRUE!

The word *volcano* comes from Vulcan, the Roman god of fire. People throughout the world have been awed by volcanic eruptions and believed them to be the work of supernatural forces.

Pyroclastic flow **is a type
of rap music with an
aggressive rhyming scheme
and sharp rhythms.**

FALSE!

A pyroclastic flow is a cloud of hot ash and gas that erupts from a volcano and travels mostly along the ground.

15

TRUE OR FALSE?

Volcanologists (scientists who study volcanoes) measure the strength of eruptions by using a scale called the Volcanic Explosivity Index (VEI).

LOW HIGH

17

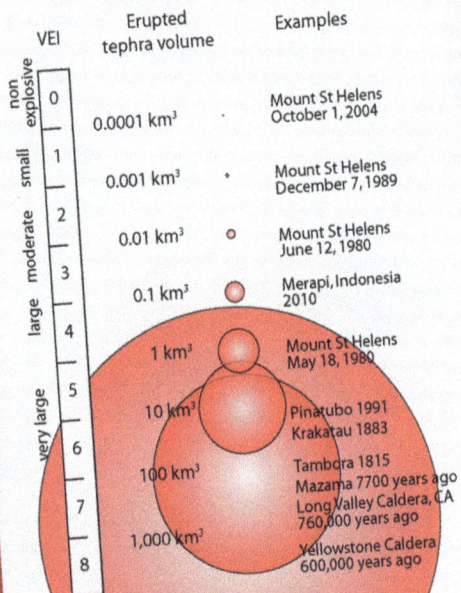

Volcanic Explosivity Index (VEI)

VEI		Erupted tephra volume		Examples
non explosive	0	0.0001 km³	·	Mount St Helens October 1, 2004
small	1	0.001 km³	·	Mount St Helens December 7, 1989
moderate	2	0.01 km³	◦	Mount St Helens June 12, 1980
	3	0.1 km³	●	Merapi, Indonesia 2010
large	4	1 km³		Mount St Helens May 18, 1980
	5	10 km³		Pinatubo 1991 Krakatau 1883
very large	6	100 km³		Tambora 1815 Mazama 7700 years ago Long Valley Caldera, CA 760,000 years ago
	7	1,000 km³		Yellowstone Caldera 600,000 years ago
	8			

TRUE!

In this explosive measurement system, eruptions are assigned numbers from 0, for the weakest, to 8, for the strongest.

TRUE OR FALSE?

Lava is the most dangerous hazard of a volcanic eruption.

FALSE!

Pyroclastic flows are the most dangerous volcanic hazard. They can choke or poison people with gases, bury them in debris, and burn them with temperatures of up to 1100 °F (600 °C). They advance tens or hundreds of feet or meters per second. They can even cross such natural barriers as rivers and ridges.

TRUE OR FALSE?

The capital of the Caribbean island of Montserrat is a volcanic ruin.

1914 1918

1945

25

TRUE!

In 1997, a volcanic eruption in the Soufriére Hills destroyed the nearby capital of Plymouth. The ghost town remains the island's legal capital, though all government business now takes place in the town of Brades Estate.

28

TRUE OR FALSE?

Volcanic eruptions can temporarily cool Earth's climate.

29

TRUE!

Huge volcanic eruptions can release large amounts of ash into the atmosphere, blocking sunlight and cooling Earth's surface. The 1991 eruption of Mount Pinatubo in the Philippines, for example, caused the average global temperature to dip 0.9 Fahrenheit degree (0.5 Celsius degree) for almost two years.

TRUE OR FALSE?

The Ring of Fire is the
most powerful ring in
The Lord of the Rings book series.

FALSE!

The Ring of Fire is a horseshoe-shaped belt along the edge of the Pacific Ocean that is home to many volcanoes and earthquakes.

But, the Ring of
Power in *The Lord of
the Rings* was forged
inside a volcano—
Mount Doom!

36

TRUE OR FALSE?

Twin volcanoes erupted
in movie theaters
everywhere in 1997.

TRUE!

Dueling disaster flicks hit the big screens in 1997. In *Volcano*, a volcano erupts in the middle of downtown Los Angeles. In *Dante's Peak*, a volcanologist tries to warn a Pacific Northwest community of a coming volcanic disaster.

40

TRUE OR FALSE?

Yellowstone National Park in Wyoming is one giant volcano.

41

TRUE!

Most of Yellowstone sits atop a complex of ancient *calderas*. A *caldera* is a crater formed by the collapse of a huge underground magma chamber. Yellowstone has not erupted since prehistoric times. But evidence suggests that its past eruptions have been among the most powerful on Earth.

TRUE OR FALSE?

Water dissolved in magma
can help cool a volcano, causing a less
explosive eruption.

45

FALSE!

As a volcano erupts, water dissolved in the magma bubbles out as steam. Magma with little dissolved water erupts fairly smoothly. But magma with lots of dissolved water bursts out violently, like a soft drink that has been shaken.

TRUE OR FALSE?

The largest known volcano
is out of this world!

48

49

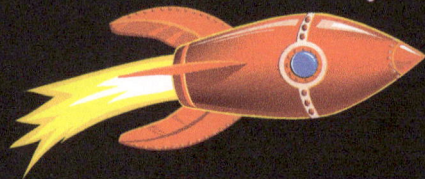

The largest known volcano
is on Mars. Olympus Mons rises
about 16 miles (25 kilometers)
above the surrounding plains.
It is more than 370 miles
(600 kilometers) in diameter.

TRUE OR FALSE?

The U.S. state of
Hawaii is made of
volcanoes.

TRUE!

Hawaii is made up of 132 islands. All the islands were formed by volcanoes built up from the ocean floor.

TRUE OR FALSE?

Volcanoes erupt square-shaped rocks called *lava cubes.*

FALSE!

But flows of lava can
leave behind hollow, cavelike
structures called
lava tubes.

TRUE OR FALSE?

Volcanoes can erupt
so powerfully that they
destroy themselves.

TRUE!

The volcanic island Krakatau in Indonesia erupted so violently in 1883 that it disappeared beneath the sea.

In 1980, an eruption of Mount Saint Helens in Washington state caused more than 1,000 feet (300 meters) of its cone to collapse.

TRUE OR FALSE?

Volcanic eruptions can disrupt air travel.

65

TRUE!

In 2010, Iceland's Eyjafjallajökull volcano erupted, releasing a gigantic ash cloud. Ash can enter and destroy jet engines, so air travel across Europe was rerouted or delayed for months.

TRUE OR FALSE?

A huge
volcanic eruption
caused the *extinction*
(dying out) of the dinosaurs.

FALSE!

(PROBABLY)

Most scientists think the dinosaurs died out when a huge asteroid collided with Earth. But, a huge volcanic eruption occurred in what is now India around the same time. The resulting lava beds, called the Deccan Traps, cover about 200,000 square miles (500,000 square kilometers), an area nearly the size of Texas.

TRUE OR FALSE?

72

Strombolian eruptions are named for stromboli, an Italian American turnover dish made with meat and cheese.

FALSE!

Strombolian eruptions produce fireworks like bursts of lava and *pyroclasts* (rock fragments). They are named for Stromboli, an island volcano off the coast of Italy that has been erupting in this way for centuries.

75

TRUE OR FALSE?

The serene-looking Mount Fuji in Japan is actually a volcano.

TRUE!

Mount Fuji is a type of volcano called a *stratovolcano*. Hundreds of eruptions over thousands of years have created its eye-pleasing shape. Fuji last erupted in 1707.

TRUE OR FALSE?

The smallest type of volcanic landform is called a *smolcano.*

FALSE!

Cinder cones are the smallest volcanic landform. Most cinder cones are active for only a few years, not long enough to build a massive peak like a stratovolcano. Cinder cones are usually only a few hundred feet or about 100 meters tall.

TRUE OR FALSE?

This *volcanologist* is helping to save lives.

TRUE!

As little as 100 years ago, people had little or no warning before a volcanic eruption. Today, volcanologists monitor volcanoes. Their work can help detect a coming eruption, giving people warning to evacuate.

87

TRUE OR FALSE?

Volcanoes called *cryovolcanoes* erupt tears when they are sad.

89

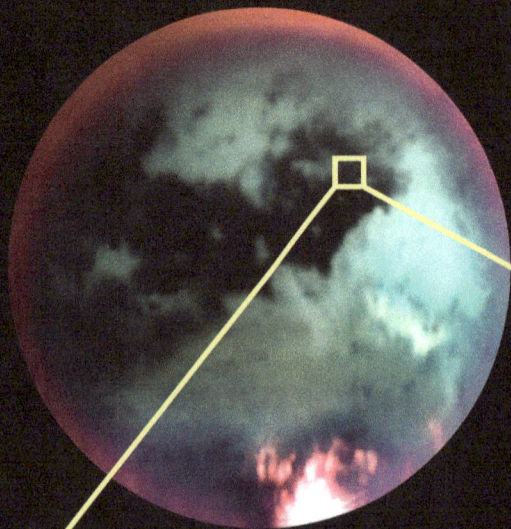

TRUE!

Cryovolcanoes are icy volcanoes that erupt water, ammonia, methane, or other substances in extremely cold temperatures. Scientists have found evidence of cryovolcanic activity on the icy moons of our solar system, including Saturn's moon Titan. (*Cryo* comes from a Greek word meaning *cold.*)

DID YOU KNOW...

In A.D. 79, the volcano Vesuvius erupted, **burying the ancient Roman cities** of Pompeii and Herculaneum.

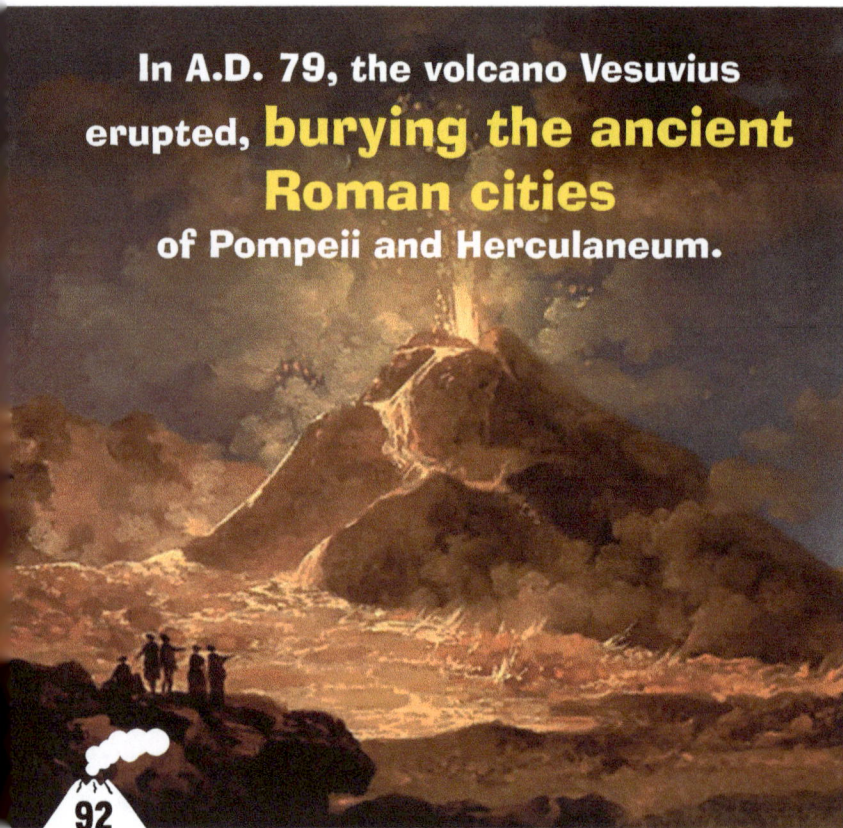

Pumice is a stone made from **frothy magma** that is flung into the air and hardens before it lands. Trapped air bubbles enable pumice to float in water!

Airborne ash from large volcanic eruptions can spread across the world, causing brilliant sunrises and sunsets for many days.

A *lahar* is a volcanic mudflow made of water and ash.

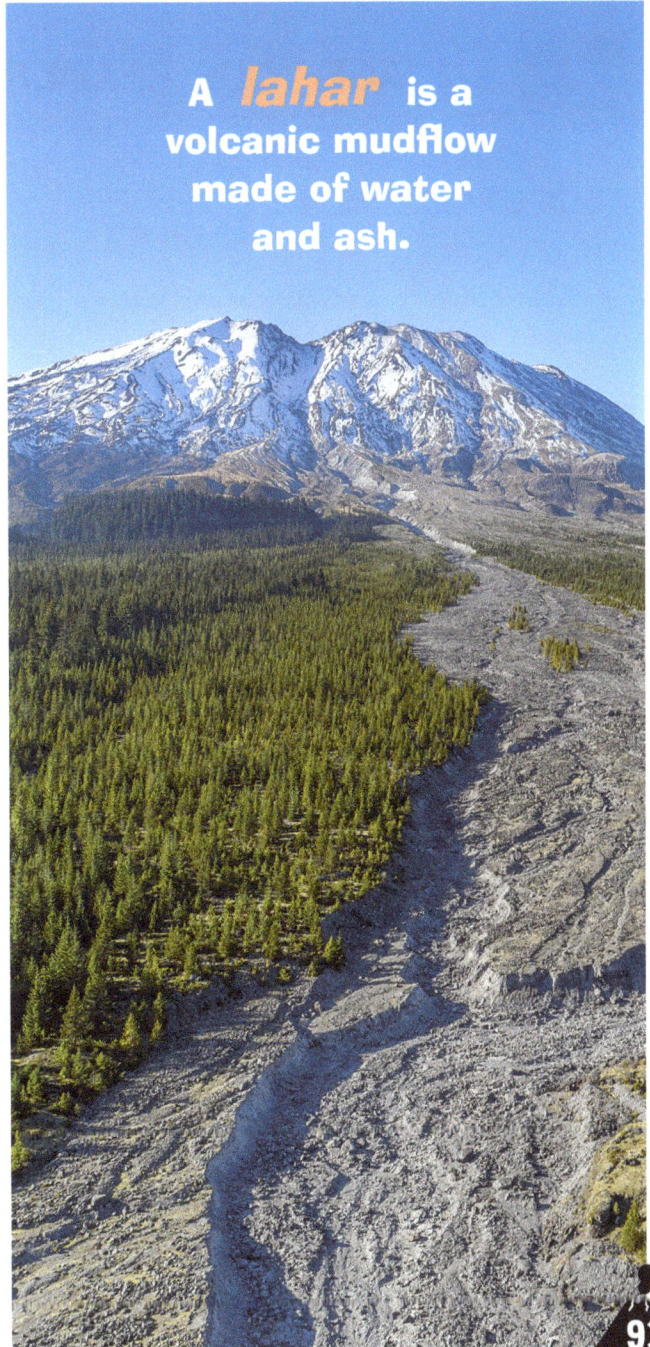

Volcanoes do not last forever. **They go extinct** if their source of magma runs out.

ENGAGE YOUR READER

GUIDED READING PROMPTS

Before Reading

- Allow readers to scan the text and discuss what they notice so far. Highlight the structure of this text and explain that the answers include both evidence and reasoning that support the claim of true or false.

- Explain the literacy skill: *Sometimes authors write a claim and then use evidence and reasoning to help make their point clear. Look for these elements as you read!*

During Reading

- Read each statement and provide time to discuss whether readers believe it to be true or false before turning the page to learn the facts.

- As you read, model how to identify the claims, evidence, and reasoning in the text. Prompt your readers to identify these features as they explore the text, too.

- Encourage readers to further discuss their learning by pausing to discuss surprising information.

After Reading

- Prompt your readers to connect, extend, and challenge their thinking about the text:
    - What will you take away from reading this text?
    - What changes in your thinking happened while reading and learning?
    - What is still challenging your thinking? What questions or wonderings do you still have?

LOOK BACK!

- Prompt readers to look back through the text to identify examples of interesting or thought-provoking claims.

- Challenge readers to explain what makes these examples so engaging.

CURRICULUM CONNECTIONS

These questions and tasks support the following English/Language Arts skills:

- Determining what a text says both explicitly and implicitly
- Citing specific evidence when drawing conclusions
- Interpreting words and phrases used in a text
- Analyzing how the structure of a text affects how it is read.

LITERACY SKILL

Authors make their claims stronger by supporting them with evidence and reasoning.

- A claim is a statement of truth.
- Evidence includes the facts or information that prove whether the claim is true.
- Reasoning includes any logical explanation that describes how the evidence supports the claim.

Example from the text: Pages 28-31

- Claim: Volcanic eruptions can temporarily cool Earth's climate.
- Evidence: Volcanic eruptions can release ash into the atmosphere.
- Reasoning: Large eruptions create enough ash to block the sun, allowing less heat to reach Earth, sometimes causing global temperatures to drop.

EXTEND THROUGH WRITING

Challenge readers to create their own True/False questions and answers about volcanoes.

- Have readers use a trusted reference, such as www.worldbookonline.com, to research information related to volcanoes. Encourage readers to look for key details, fun facts, or surprising features that would make strong True or False statements.
- Give readers one notecard for each claim they research.
- Direct readers to write the claim on the front of the notecard. On the back, readers should describe why that claim is true or false using evidence and reasoning from their research.

MORE WAYS TO ENGAGE!

- Play a game! After considering each claim, have readers signify "true" with a thumb up and "false" with a thumb down. Keep score to see who knows their facts about volcanoes the best!
    - Develop collaboration skills by grouping readers together into teams.
- Further discuss any True/False claims that revealed readers' misconceptions. Focus the conversation on *why* they initially thought what they did and how the text helped them learn.

Acknowledgments

Cover © Roman Samborskyi, Shutterstock; © Ekaterina Mikhaylova, Shutterstock

4-21 © Shutterstock
22-23 Peter Lipman, United States Geological Survey
24-25 © Rolf Richardson, Alamy Images
26-27 © Photovolcanica.com/ Shutterstock; © Andrew Woodley, Alamy Images
28-32 © Shutterstock
34-35 © Science Photo Library/Alamy Images
36-37 © Shutterstock
38-39 © Zasimov Yurii, Shutterstock; © Universal Pictures; © 20th Century Fox
40-42 © Shutterstock
44-45 © Bakavets Sviatlana, Shutterstock; © mauritius images GmbH/Alamy Images
46-47 © Bakavets Sviatlana, Shutterstock; © mktordonez/iStock
48-49 © Shutterstock
50-51 © Stocktrek Images/Alamy Images
52-53 © Maridav/Shutterstock

54-55 © MN Studio/Shutterstock; United States Geological Survey
56-57 © 3d-sparrow/Shutterstock
58-59 © Arctic Images/Alamy Images
60-61 United States Geological Survey; © Anak Tinta, Shutterstock
62-63 Public Domain; United States Geological Survey; © Shutterstock
64-82 © Shutterstock
84-86 United States Geological Survey
88-89 © Shutterstock
90-91 NASA
92-93 Eruption of Vesuvius, 14th of Mai 1771 (1771), oil on canvas by Pierre-Jacques Volaire; Staatliche Kunsthalle Karlsruhe; © Cesar Santana, Alamy Images; © Shutterstock
94 © ShiipArt/Shutterstock; © NeMaria/Shutterstock